LIVING AT THE MONASTERY, WORKING IN THE KITCHEN

Also by Eric Paul Shaffer

kindling: Poems from Two Poets (Longhand Press; co-author, James Taylor III)

RattleSnake Rider (Longhand Press)

How I Read Gertrude Stein by Lew Welch (Grey Fox Press)

Instant Mythology (Backer Editions)

Portable Planet (Leaping Dog Press)

LIVING AT THE MONASTERY, WORKING IN THE KITCHEN

POEMS

Eric Paul Shaffer

For Elizabeth —
I hope you enjoy the long,
loud laughter of Shih-te!

Best,
Eric

LEAPING DOG
P·R·E·S·S

Chantilly, Virginia : 2001

Grateful acknowledgment is extended to the following magazines, which originally published some of these poems: *Chaminade Literary Review, Chiron Review, Fish Drum, Grain, Nightsun, Parnassus Literary Review, Poetry Motel, Prose Ax, Real Good Stuff,* and *Threepenny Review.*

ISBN 1-58775-004-X (paper)
ISBN 1-58775-005-8 (electronic)
Library of Congress Control Number: 2001092191

This book has been printed on recycled, acid-free paper, by McNaughton & Gunn, Saline, MI, and has been published in an edition of 1,200 copies, of which the first 100 are signed and numbered by the author.

This is number _____ of 100.

Paperback original, Leaping Dog Press Book #3.
Cover art by Andrew Shkolnik.
Chinese calligraphy by Lian Wan.
Cover design by Jordan Jones and Eric Paul Shaffer.

Leaping Dog Press
PO Box 222605
Chantilly, VA 20153-2605
www.leapingdogpress.com

Acknowledgments

There is no way to indicate the dimensions of my debt to Red Pine, a.k.a. Bill Porter, concerning the conception and composition of these poems. His interest and enthusiasm for the work, his many books of translations of Chinese poets and his interviews with Chinese monks, his willingness to answer questions of all shapes and sizes, is thoroughly and gratefully acknowledged here. I also owe much to the work of John Blofeld, Robert G. Henricks, Kenneth Rexroth, Gary Snyder, Arthur Waley, Burton Watson, Mike O'Connor, Paul Hansen, James Hargett, James Sanford, J. P. Seaton, Paul Kahn, and many others for their fine translations, notes, prefaces, introductions, and appendices, and the insights they provided. I encourage all readers to explore the poems these translators make available to us. The work of these writers, translators, and scholars was essential in the composition of my poems, but no matter how much of the success of these lines is the result of their excellence, I am solely responsible for faults or errors.

I send warmest greetings and owe greatest thanks to these eminent humans: Veronica Winegarner, Jordan Jones, Red Pine, Jim Harrison, Sara Backer, Steve Sanfield, John Kain, James Taylor III, Cheri Crenshaw, Andrew Shkolnik, David Robertson, P. D. Murphy, Sean O'Grady, Suzi Winson, Cold Peak, Big Shield, Pick Up, and the rest of the *Ancient Order of the Fire Gigglers.*

INSTRUCTIONS: Do your work. Stop. Listen. Eat. Wash your bowl. Sit still. Breathe.

Send comments, complaints, and *koans* to eshaffer@hotmail.com.

Contents

On the Steps of the Temple

T welve summers ago, on the roof of the *Damnation,* my friend John's antique houseboat on the Sacramento River, I sat in the sun reading *Cold Mountain Poems,* Gary Snyder's translations of twenty-four of the 307 surviving works of Han-shan. That day, I drowsed over the woodcut of Han-shan and an anonymous companion I assumed was Shih-te. I wondered about Shih-te. Surely, he was as much a madman as Han-shan. Where were his poems? With that mystery in mind, I leaped from the roof into the river. When I climbed back on deck, I found paper and pen in the cabin and quickly wrote five short poems for Shih-te, in what I hoped was his voice.

Three years later, in Taipei, I met up again with Red Pine, a.k.a. Bill Porter, translator of Chinese poetry and interviewer of contemporary Chinese monks. On a tour of the National Palace Museum, I mentioned my interest in Shih-te. Bill led me to paintings of the two madmen of the cloudy peak. Not only did he assure me that Shih-te had not been silent, but later, at his home at Bamboo Lake, he presented me with a copy of *On Temple Walls,* a beautiful hand-bound book of his own translations of Shih-te's complete works. I read the forty-nine poems with glee, admiring Shih-te's rough and reckless spirit, his crazy crankiness, his gruff, plain words, his touchy grumpiness with people and life, his sudden and surprising thoughts and acts, ranging from barbs to blows. I read the poems often, disappointed only that there were no more.

The next year, it was May in Okinawa, where I taught English composition and American conversation to Japanese students at the University of the Ryukyus. I was attending a faculty meeting, but with my limited grasp of Japanese, I was lost in the proceedings. I had my cup of green tea and my photo-copied handouts, but I couldn't read them, so I passed the time studying the characters on the pages and the view through the windows. Half the faculty seemed asleep or drowsing. Some read. Others stared into space, and a few carried on the meeting, debating issues clearly of consequence. As I gazed over cane fields and *deigo* trees at the distant Pacific, I thought of Shih-te. The eighth-century T'ang Dynasty cook and janitor living in a Chinese mountain monastery, a man amidst but not among, at once within and without, was, in an amusing and intriguing way, in a situation much like mine at the university; for two men with hundreds of miles and years between us, we shared some common ground.

After riding the bus home, I unearthed my original five Shih-te poems and began to compose more. The task became a devotion and daily meditation during the eight years I lived on the edge of Asia. *Living at the Monastery, Working in the Kitchen,* then, is a collection of poems written in the voice of Shih-te, resident cook and janitor at Kuo-ch'ing Temple in the T'ien-t'ai mountains of eighth-century China during the T'ang Dynasty and companion to the renowned Han-shan. These poems are works without provenance, originals of unknown origins, what I call, for want of a better term, "textless translations."

EPS
April 1, 2001
on the sunset slope of Haleakala, Maui

Dust from the Broom:
Literary, Historical, &
Legendary Background

S hih-te was the close companion of Han-shan, legendary Chinese poet of the T'ang Dynasty who lived on a peak in the T'ien-t'ai Mountains. Shih-te lived in Kuo-ch'ing, a nearby Buddhist-Taoist monastery. Lost, abandoned, or orphaned as a young boy, Shih-te was brought to the monastery by Feng-kan, another resident monk, who had found him. Working in the kitchen, Shih-te apparently showed little respect for the monks for whom he cooked and cleaned, but he saved scraps and rags for Han-shan, who visited regularly. The two men were wild together, and seated in the kitchen, they laughed and joked about the *dharma* to which others devoted themselves with silent meditation, riddles, and daily labor within the halls and the temple grounds around them. Despite their noisy irreverence, the two were allowed the run of the monastery and environs, much to the displeasure of the other monks, and the fame of Han-shan and Shih-te grew, even during their lifetimes. Feng-kan noted that the rowdy pair knew more of the Way than most monks and masters in residence, so as the famed preface to the poems of Han-shan indicates, when Lu-ch'iu Yin, the governor of the prefecture, came to pay his respects to the two friends as they sat in the kitchen one day, they ridiculed him and ran away. A literary and folk tradition regarding the two as unschooled yet enlightened men arose around the circulation of poems attributed to Han-shan, Shih-te, and Feng-kan. Over three hundred poems credited to Han-shan survive, with fewer than half a hundred of Shih-te and four of Feng-kan, though accurate attribution of many is still debated.

Dates for the lives of Shih-te, Han-shan, and Feng-kan are difficult to determine. The early eighth century is a traditional and popular era in which to place the lives of these men, but dates for the famed meeting of Shih-te, Han-shan, and Lu-ch'iu Yin in the kitchen of Kuo-ch'ing Monastery range from 633 to 800 A.D. For none but literary reasons, I prefer early T'ang dates, but a lively, amusing, and illuminating debate among scholars and translators continues.

Little is known of the daily lives of Shih-te, Han-shan, and Feng-kan, and since I know even less of the circumstances of mountain monastery life in China twelve or thirteen centuries ago, the poems of the three men have been the trailheads for my departures into the bewilderness that produces poems. I have also drawn largely on the prefaces, introductions, and notes in the many translations of Chinese poetry I have read as part of my work. I wish I could say that I have stuck closely to the "facts" of Shih-te's life and thought as I explored them in my poems, but since the facts are indeterminate at best, I've used the compass of inspiration and taken directions others might ignore or avoid. I have read widely and wildly, well beyond the dynasty of the T'ang and the cliffs of T'ien-t'ai, in order to envision Shih-te as he lived and worked. To the discerning reader, it will be evident that these poems are written in a spirit that disregards the equally imaginary borders of countries and centuries.

A Note on the Names

Among the many ways that the work, translations, and scholarship of Bill Porter affect this book is a fundamental feature of Shih-te: his name. Porter renders the name of Shih-te, known as *Jittoku* in Japanese, as "Pick Up." Earthy and ambiguous, the name stuck with me, and I savored it. As a result, the significance of names and naming became fundamental to my conception of Shih-te and definitive of his character, actions, ideas, and concerns as he inhabited my poems.

I also employ Porter's translation of Feng-kan, known as *Bukan* in Japanese, as "Big Shield." In *The Collected Songs of Cold Mountain* (2000), a new revised and expanded edition of the poems of Han-shan, which also includes all of the poems of Feng-kan and Shih-te, Porter has changed his translation of the name of Feng-kan to "Big Stick," a reference to the unusual height of the monk. So many of my poems were composed based on the first translation that I retain Porter's original choice, even as I reserve the right to revise throughout the third millennium.

For my own reasons, however, I refer to Han-shan, known as *Kanzan* in Japanese, as "Cold Peak," instead of the more familiar "Cold Mountain" or "Cold Cliff."

Living at the Monastery, Working in the Kitchen

•

The night Big Shield found me freezing
in the white maw of a blizzard,
my legs were numb,
my fingers frozen, bent into hooks
for coaxing blood through my body.

He laughed loudly,
and I woke
to his legs, dark columns to the clouds.

Bending low to clasp my claw,
he hoisted me
onto his back, high above the drifts.

"Come, little one," he laughed again,
"you still have work to do."

•

●

Words wind from my mouth
    as hair winds from my head—
thick, shiny, tough lines of black
    that dirty with the dust of days,
    knot, tangle, and fall.

    The bald monks grimace
when they find my poems on walls,
        on leaves, in mud, on rock,
as though seeing a single strand of black
    in an evening bowl of rice.

●

●

"Whose child?"

        "Whose child is this?"

As sparrows to a hawk,

      the monks chattered at Big Shield

dropping me to the hard floor of the temple.

     "Yours,"

        he replied,

striding back into the snowstorm.

That was the only night the monks ever cared

              for me—

when they thought I would be gone

      the next day.

●

●

Sparrows scatter at my step
but gather round to teach
                    when I sit still.

They leap through leaves and pebbles,
seeking morsels, but the seed a sparrow finds
                    is luck
and bitter persistence, and still he looks.

The sparrow expects nothing
and finds enough.

How can I crave more?

The sparrow sees
we deserve nothing at all,
                    but look
at all we find.

●

●

That nosy governor follows me everywhere,
a tall, red dust rising from my tracks.

Listening to my little grunts,
catching idle comments to Fire Boy,
he records noisy ignorance
in sloppy characters of ink.

All day, he gazes my way, concealing paper and brush.

"Ho!"

At my shout, he leaps like carp
in white pools where water cascades from clouds.
He claims he writes
so others may benefit.

How brave to record my words
just so
scholars may say they know better.

●

Lu-ch'iu Yin, new governor of the province which included the T'ien-t'ai Mountains, visited Kuo-ch'ing Temple to meet Han-shan and Shih-te, whom he had heard from Feng-kan were among the enlightened, but the two realized the governor's intentions to "record their wisdom," ridiculed him, and ran away.

●

Cold Peak and I found the old man
dangling skinny legs wrapped in rags

over a sheer granite drop

to shadows and green below.

Laughing at the edge, waving arms through blue,

he spurned our help, our words.
Hungry, he refused even rice we offered,

cried he would step into the heavens

if we came too near.

His eldest son had led him to the cliff

but had no heart

to shove him over … and left him there,

but the old man's gladness shone

as sun glows on stone.

"All for nothing," he giggled,
"All for nothing."

●

One ancient practice, in China and many other parts of the world, was to lead elderly people into the wilderness and abandon them. This practice was considered a humane way to deal with the difficulties posed by the old and infirm.

●

These lazy monks
raise robes to piss in streams
draining to parched throats
on the dusty yellow plains below.

There is no teaching these grinning fools.
They stare at my shouts and think
me crazy.

The Old Master was a buddha
to undertake such a task.

I'd rather talk to temple dogs
and grow vegetables from excrement.

●

●

By the red pine on the verge
of the garden,
magpie, big noisy bird of black and white,
sheen of rainbow on walking wings,

squawks at windy limbs, falling cones,
glowing boulders,
and the bald skulls of brown monks
sweeping stones.

●

●

"It is customary to leave an offering
of food
on the rim of one's plate
in respect for other worlds."

The old kitchen monk
wagged a wooden tongue and serving stick
above my unruly head.

"Sir," I said, "I hunger,
and I will make no offerings
to worlds I cannot see,
for if I thought there were more worlds
than this,
I would not dare eat at all."

●

●

Cold Peak stepped from the trees
　　　with long hair and little clothing

singing something
　　　I couldn't quite hear,
　　　　　　　singing something.

I never saw his eyes turn to me
　　　when I finally spoke as we sat on grass,
　　　"Looks like you're the only one here
　　　　　　I can talk to."

He laughed but said nothing.

That day too the sun set,
　　　but I don't remember when.

●

●

From the shore of the sea, comes a monk
with a weathered gray tooth the size of a peach pit.

In a tempest, his grandfather wrestled wind,

rain, and crashing waves,
and tore the tooth
from a raging dragon's jaw.

The monks are agog with blank-eyed wonder.

The tooth may come from the mouth of a dragon,
but the tale comes from the tongue of a fool.

●

●

Big Shield made my name a joke.
              He called me "Pick Up."

The monks misunderstood,
                     thinking me the one
          to clean up after them
          only literally.

●

•

The Buddha left a palace
to lose himself in the world,
to wander under sky and stars for seven years,
to sit at last among tangled roots.

Monks linger in temples longer
and loiter
till enlightenment.

Where is the wonder
they rarely see?

•

●

One evening in the kitchen,
cooking for monks, I sang a poem.
With no tinder or kindling,

I stuffed leaves in the stove,
and lit a little ball of words
to catch the wood.

I barely remember the poem:

"What we call poetry is only words.
Let them not linger long in the air
or on the page,

lest they grow great in some future
eye or ear
desperate for an imaginary golden age,

and we become merely gods
magnified by distance
and the delusions of our descendants."

Usually, lines that stick in the mind
and live on the tongue
are better ones.

●

●

Books! Monks and books!

All day long reading aloud,
                    droning dead words smarter
                                    than they are.

What do they mean with all this noise?

The day the old Master stacked the library on the grass
                    and set the pages burning
        he used a single flame.

Mine was the only hand clapping.

●

●

All seem to know me here.
The Porch of Heaven rings with a name
                    Big Shield gave me years ago.

Pick Up's the name I'm known by,
          and it's just as well. If there's another,
          it's long gone now.

In the foolish abbot's face, I shout,
          "But how do you know me?"

He stands on his shadow and sputters,
                    "I see your face every day. I know
          your name. I recognize you."

Even Cold Peak thinks he knows me
          at a glance.

Clearly, I am lost.

Whether I see this face
                    in pail or pool,
          I don't know who I see.

How could I look like that man?
I don't even resemble myself.

●

●

The Way is open and free,
wide as a rice patty in Spring,
silver and broad as the face of brown water,
and unguarded as a pearl

in an oyster's open mouth, shimmering
in sunlight, among starfish and green weeds.
Yet we dare not reach
for what is free, for fear

of the unknown, the expected,
imagined menace lying
at the lip of freedom.
Instead, we cower and retreat

like an army fleeing the gaping gates
of an undefended city, only because
Kung Ming in robe and slippers
glowers from atop the wall.

●

Kung Ming was a brilliant strategist of warfare. Legend has it that he turned aside an invading army for which he was unprepared by throwing open the city gates and sitting in plain view atop the walls. He was recognized by the approaching forces, who feared a trap and fled.

·

Cold Peak pouts.

The man who walks alone is truly alone
only when none note his solitude.

With no eye to see him, Cold Peak simply wanders
blank and open to the blue,
so I raise mine to gray cliffs and watch for him.

The solitary life of Cold Peak proves
one may live long on the Edge of Heaven,
falling neither in
nor out.

●

•

The kitchen I work in is dark,

                but clean as a kernel of raw rice.

My broom stands by the stove,

                palm-polished wood in easy reach

should I wish to sweep red dust around the room.

A white monkey in gray branches rustling

                outside the kitchen window

    in the breeze through every afternoon

        inspires me.

At sunset, I steam fresh rice on the stove

        to tweak the noses of sitting monks,

            reeling in a cosmos on the hook

                of a scent.

        What I practice,

          I practice

            every day.

The monks sit silent and swallow often.

•

•

"The crane lives for a thousand years
        and its call is as constant as day."

Monks grumble
when they scrub such lines from temple walls.

One whines, "Why must these wild men
              make work for us
while we seek the way?"

"Why does the abbot allow
        such nonsense?" wails another.

Wash the walls well, silly students,
           learn your lessons,
    and do not wonder
    at words you wipe away.

The crane lives for a thousand years
and is never silent once.

•

In China, the crane is an ancient symbol of longevity. As cranes migrate, they gather by the thousands, and since their calls never stop, the sound is truly majestic.

●

The Head Monk secretly cherishes his shadow.
　　　　Darkness dogs his every step,
　　and he winks when he thinks
　　　　　no one sees.

　　At night, his shadow vanishes,
　　　　　　and he is lost.

Seeking the outhouse,
　　　　　he crashes through the kitchen,
　　　　toppling utensils and bumping bowls.

Outside, he curses staggering
　　　　　　through my vegetables
　　or trudges sullenly through
　　　　　the gravel in the monks' garden.

　　I turn on my pallet behind the stove,
　　　　　and I do not rise to help.

　　Even pointing is pointless
　　　　　for those seeking shadows
　　　　　　lost in moonlight.

●

●

The blazing din of summer
　　　　splits the ragged cliff.

Bright banners hang limp
　　　　　　in the sun.

The dull bronze curve
　　　　　of the temple bell
is silent, but cool to the cheek.

In the hall, monks dream
　　　　　of immortality
　　　　with the shrill song

of ten thousand cicadas
　　　　ringing in their ears.

●

●

Among pines and boulders,
the path is clearest
when there is no place to go,

for through clouds and cliffs,
one goes nowhere
when there is no place to go,

and one can go nowhere
till he knows the path, too,
is a place.

●

●

A man with copper, silver, and gold
knotted on strings around his neck
will never raise his eyes to see,
let alone climb, the Lotus Peak.

Heels in rutted mud,
eyes on a narrow path through ricefields,
from where he stands,
only birds fly to heaven.

And only hermits are crazy enough to climb.

●

●

Most days I refuse
Cold Peak's invitation to the clouds.

Not that I have much to do
but gaze on the little model of the world
            young monks tend in the yard,
    laboring in a garden of rock and swept stone.

In the kitchen, fire cooks rice
but only with the willing work of water.
I am happy as I am,
            and that's enough.

As we leave all thoughts, let us leave all things—
    as they are, in their places.

No need to climb up or down
            for a view of the world
    within the world.
Here, one smells rice steaming,

hears the mealtime tap and clunk
            of sticks and bowls, tastes the high
    chill of peaks in waters
rushing through rock from blue heights.

●

●

No one asks me
for my answer, yet I have none.

I watch monks wrestle hard words,
sweat over riddles
set between two ears
on nodding heads thick as temple gates.

Not even a brick
will summon the sleeper within.

●

Fire Boy talks to himself,

        all morning, trimming wicks for lamps.

"If we could run fast enough,

        we might always live in daylight

        and never need lamps.

        What a bright day that would be!"

Sounds too much like too much work—

        for this ragged janitor, at least.

And if one could run that fast,

        he'd better stay in one place

        and learn the pace of day.

●

When Big Shield drew his house on his wall,
I said, "Now, it is clear.
The picture is in the house."

He said nothing.

Now, I see the image ravaged by rain and rats,
weather and winter,
long after the man is gone.

Indeed, one might well say,
"The house is in the picture."

All things contain all things.

●

●

Through the old master's window,
I hear monks mumble

stumbling words of private answers.
He is silent.

He often kneels in garden mud with me
and pulls weeds in morning light.

It's a pity
to pity these poor bald boys.

Faced with a closed door in moonlight,
not one could choose to push or to knock.

●

The words "to push or to knock" recall the famous meeting of Ji Dao and Han Yu. Xiang Su records that the two became friends when Han Yu assisted Ji Dao in choosing the right word for a troublesome line of poetry.

●

A crow in flight
brushes a black line through blue.

Ants creep in lines
through swept dirt on a kitchen floor.

Monks rake waves
through gray morning gravel.

I wash rice in a wooden pail.

I have nothing
but work
to do.

●

•

At an age now when my back
is stiff and bowed as an old broomshaft,
I dream of the dirt hut
where I was born.

My dreams are drab—
picking at scabs
from scratching at the bites of the matbugs—
and I wake from short nights
scratching at new scabs
on thin old legs.

I will leave a pot of rice steaming
and die even as I have lived—
where I am, here—
living at the monastery,
working in the kitchen.

•

●

Alas, young monks weep
　　　　at sudden news of death,
birth, marriage, and other accidents
　　　　　　in the plains below the peaks.

They cast rain to the clouds.

On the Ledge of Heaven,
　　　we are all orphans.

Such news means nothing—
　not to monks, not to crazy hermits,
　　　　not to this cook,
tossed, too young, into snow and midnight.

It's all refuse swept from the kitchen chopblock—
　knots cut from carrots, shucked husks of rice,
　　　　and mushy hearts in green leaves
　stored too long and long gone bad.

●

●

Big Shield once told me all
may be enlightened:
serpent, stone, bell, moon, pine.

Imagine that.

Yet, my question remains:
"On what great day
will fear and hope finally die?"

"Back to work,"
said Big Shield.
"Even the sun must climb Cold Peak."

●

●

Who works to be free
will never be free.

Raise two hands to your eyes.
Show yourself your bonds.
You see nothing.

Pity those bound by a whisper of wishes.

You are free
only when you forget
you are free.

If you seek freedom,
desire binds you,
and you are not free.

You are free.

●

●

The glory of this great round moon
would make the Buddha gasp.

Stars shy from silver light
framed by soft black boughs
in a sky so deep in blue
a lone cloud sails dark crests on an empty sea.

What a shame to say all this
just because I can't
keep my mouth shut.

●

●

Not a monk here heeds me,
even when I glare
like stone lions guarding temple gates.

I walk narrow halls
with no more substance than the shadow of a man
swallowed by the shadow of a cloud.

Big Shield alone marks me
among the rustle and rasp of robes
as the other one with wild hair and eyes.

If it weren't for him,
I'd be working in a kitchen
somewhere else.

●

●

Young monks gaped in awe
when the old master came to meals but never ate.

Their fear was funny.
They whispered of hungry ghosts, magic kettles,
and lost desires of the holy.
I teased them with tales of one-eyed demons rising in the dark.

One night, I caught the old master
at the trap in the drain where rice gathers
when monks wash their bowls
after the evening meal.

No more rice than would fill a hermit's thimble,
yet the old monk carried
his portion to a spot warmed by the stove
and ate his meal with simple grace.

Such is the way.
Numbskulls never tire of stuffing empty heads
with grain too good for them,
while the wise survive on scraps
left by a sullen cleansing of bowls and sticks.

One wishes
the mouths of fools might open
only to shove in rice.

●

●

Money may one day buy the moon,
but my peace is priceless.

I would say nay to any sky-eyed merchant,
be he man, god, or ghost.

Neither wish nor will can change the truth:
none buy what none desire.

What I have costs not one copper coin.
Desire is the price of freedom.

●

●

With no Master,
I have none to visit
in Autumn, when wind blows
six-petaled blossoms from the West.

Under only clouds and stars,
I lie on steps before the kitchen door,
fart and scratch myself
like any Buddha.

●

●

The governor wears nice clothes,
　　　　　　but for a man of power,
　　　he is too gullible to believe.

　　By the kitchen fire,
he bowed to Cold Peak and me,
　　　and I smacked his ass with my broom.

　Cold Peak giggled. "One smart enough
　　　　　to survive the capital
　　　must work twice as hard here."

　　We both laughed loudly.
The governor only rubbed his smarting parts
　　　　　and recorded our words.

　　Such characters are hard to read,
　　　　no matter how clear
　　　the strokes of the brush.

●

●

After we woke,
on the day lightning struck
the pine in whose shade we sat,
my ears rang for hours
with the long, loud laughter of Cold Peak.

●

●

Secretly, I trailed along that morning
my mother was hauled to the steep-walled ravine
            for dumping the corpses of the poor.

    The cart clattered through sun
                on two tracks faint in a weedy path,
and the wind announced our destination
            long before wheels stopped keening.

        The shaggy driver cursed,
grunting as he threw his burden down.
                        I heard a thick stick snap,
    and a wood spoon stirred in a pot of clay.

    As creaking wheels faded, I crept to the edge
                alone. Hand over mouth and nose,
    I gazed on humanity tangled below,
                intimate and corrupt,

    becoming one with the earth and each other,
            yet each one
                alone among the others.

    The stench rises and remains with me still.

●

●

The moon, a pearl—
what crap!

Nightly, monks stand in the yard and stare
beyond the world
at what glows dumbly in darkness.

The origin of light
reflected from that changing, empty face

is ten thousand times as bright, burns colors
through earth and sky, lights the way
so clearly only a fool can lose the path.

A wise man sees the sun
is too bright to watch
and works by light whose source he never seeks.

●

●

Big Shield was moody as the sky.
His names shifted like clouds on cliffs.
Other monks feared him,
and he lived alone in a small reed hut,
a good distance from the temple.

Roaring rumbled within the woven walls.
The whole place shook,
sometimes rising into the air and spinning,
scattering sparks,
bluing the sky with the magic of solitude.

He once showed me
the inside—
golden bamboo woven with golden reeds
hung with the weapons of a soldier—
sword, short blade, helmet,

and big shield—a name he was
once known by—
a great, gently-curving metal disk
with a dragon
not painted on its face.

●

●

In a world of green rushes,
yellow springs, red dust, blue sky,
one need taste a peach only once
to know the savor.

●

In China, the "yellow springs" was a common euphemism for death; "red dust" was a familiar refer-
ence to the delusions of the senses. The peach was a symbol of immortality.

47

●

Carrying ash from kitchen coals to the great heap out back,
I watched young monks gather after evening rice
in a clearing by the outhouse.
They pointed with childish, fearful cries
at a comet arcing over the Dragon's back.

One in a voice loud with the night said,
"Ancients say 'broom stars' sweep away
the old to make way for the new."
By starlight, I saw the blunt luster of bald heads
bobbing in the dark.

Like fat carp they were, thick backs breaking
a shallow surface, rushing over mossy stones to feed on scraps.

In a voice they hadn't heard
since the old master died last spring,
I crept behind them and barked, "Ho!"
The idiots bolted like frightened horses fleeing
a snaky coil of hemp curled in mud.

Fools! If a comet swept clear the walk
for every holy one born, for every throne lost, for every river
raised by rain, the sky would never be dark,
the heavens would sing with a rasp of brooms,
and dust would fly like summer stars.

●

In China, a comet, with its feathery trailing tail, is known as a "broom star." The broom, a familiar attribute of Shih-te, is also a symbol of immortality.

●

By Maple Bridge, beyond the temple walls,
          a blind man mistook me
      for one of these shabby brown beggars.

I stole his cane and beat him with it,
          chanting sutras with the blows.

Stomping through thick red mud,
         as I left, I spat in his eye
         for good measure.

Who calls me a monk
         can go to hell.

●

●

Pine grips the earth.
Magpie grasps a single limb.
More or less is impossible.

I am the cook. I keep the kitchen.
I boil rice, gather wood, wash pots,
grow vegetables,
sweep the floor, stoke the stove.

What else is there to do?

The one who keeps the kitchen
is the cook.

●

●

Fireboy dotes on the tale of Yen Shih
and his artificial metal man from the West.

"Such a one could sweep the temple,
cook the rice, trim the wicks,
and free all from the drudgery of days."

What can I say?

None learns from work
unless he works.

Even those who work hardest
have yet to learn.

●

Though he arrived from the distant west, Yen Shih is revered in China as a master among artisans of machines and mechanical devices, in this case, a robot. His creation, constructed of ceramics, gems, and metal, however, was so life-like that it had to be dismantled before the Emperor would believe it was not human.

●

As they bathe,
these boys are honest.

Splashing, laughing, washing
only dirt away.

Skin and muscles gleam.
Water finds a way

everywhere
it streams.

If only this joy
were found
carrying water and chopping wood.

●

The last line alludes to a well-known maxim concerning the Tao: "The wondrous Tao consists in carrying water and chopping wood."

●

Monks speak of fishing,
　　　　　　　but what they say
they angle for is nothing
　　　　　　　I ever caught.

The last time I went fishing,
　　　　　　　I hooked nothing
　　　　　　　but fish
and glimpsed a crazy man with wild hair
　　　　　　　grinning up
　　　　from the bottom of the pond.

●

●

Names are empty.
Even the Emperor can change one.
Just like that.

After centuries, in a single day,
this noisy monastery became a "Realm of Serenity,"
a "Peaceful Kingdom"
on the tongue of a monk.

There is no other name
for the Terrace of Heaven.

●

●

Original face. One hand clapping. Bow-wow!
The riddle is not known for its answer.

The Savage River thunders from the peaks.
The river is not named for grassy banks on the plains.

The Way glistens on the crests of the coiling sea.
The Way is not sought for the peace we find.

And it is best not to speak of Buddhas
to one who daily watches monks eat.

●

●

When Cold Peak brags
          none understands him,
                    he forgets one,
     maybe more, who do.

Such is the way
          the wind blows:
the breeze that carries our scent
     reveals our presence.

●

The true magic of the magic pearl
　　　　　remains ever idle,
for those who possess it,
　　　possess nothing.

Those who lack it, want it, and seeking,
　　　　　find only wind and clouds,
yet those who have it,
　　　hold it naught.

●

•

Of thousands of poems
I've scrawled
on walls, on wood, in dirt, in mud, on rock,
my favorite was my worst.

That poem is lost.

Yet even those who never saw a single stroke
know every character.

•

●

Cold Peak lectures summer grasses
on The Way
and disputes The Power with a bear
who shares his sheer sunny cliff.

His crazy laughter is a sutra
for the wind.

Often, I see him beaming
at the full moon as though gazing
on a pearl, a perfect mirror
of his enlightenment.

With broom, pails of water,
buckets of rice, and a hot stove,
I gaze at the garden I cultivate
for vegetables we share.

If Cold Peak had a job,
he might be more humble.

●

●

Only fools fear Yama.

The living need fear no Judge of the Dead,
and the dead need fear no judge,

for who can harm the dead?

None need sit facing a wall in sunlight
to see karma is dogma for fools

and the fools who drive them.

It's a pity death comes
even for those
not fit to live.

●

●

So many poor bald boys believe
enlightenment
permanent.

Nothing is.

My candle flickers
in a breeze
blowing red dust
through the kitchen.

●

●

Cold Peak, my brother,
your broken, yellow bones litter
        stones at Cold Cliff's foot.

The last time I saw you
        was the last time I saw you.

The moon come and gone three times
        since then,
yet what remains of you gleams on green and gray
        in beams of sun through summer clouds.

I catch myself on the question
I came to ask you:
        "How came you here?"

I should ask myself instead.

●

●

There are many ways to the Lotus Peak.
Each finds a path to suit his steps,
                    and none sees others
from the way one walks.

All paths converge at the peak.

From the plains, the mountain grants
                a single trail to climb,
yet the peak reveals the ways are many,
though one chooses only one.

●

•

My pail of raw rice
is the cluttered mind of a monk.

With an idle finger, I draw
figures and characters,
        and the lines remain
till I clear the surface
            with an open hand.

        After the meal,
every cooked grain
            sticks to a hand
sweeping through the rice pot,
tracing the inner curve
            of emptiness.

I am a grain of rice
stuck to the tip of a finger
        pointing to the moon.

•

●

Squatting in sunlight at the kitchen door,
this old broom-steward amuses himself with names.

Fire Boy believes my memory
drifts from me in clouds

as steam steals water
from boiling rice,

but I use any word any way I please,
for why use one when any other will do?

Sought with the wrong name,
is a broom any less a broom?

Known by many names,
am I not the one who daily sweeps the temple?

Addressed as beggar or saint,
does monk or cook become more or less?

I even call the one-eared dog Big Shield
but only when monks are near enough to hear.

●

●

Within temple walls, young monks labor daily
on a garden of rock and pebbled waves,
a little model of the world.

Peak and sea!

The entire world in waves and stone—
just as they imagine.

●

●

In the kitchen, cooks cook.

                    That's what I do anyway.

Rice simmers, ah, and the smell is green. Pines.
Moss on my rock.

                    Leaves in the sun in the stream.
Wild, green, roaring, enclosing and expansive.

                    There is nature.

Outside, monks shuffle through dust,

               eyes on earth, thought
crushed, caught, tossed, lost

               the way they're taught.

Discipline, study, stillness, control.

                  There is practice.

And, here, there is a second nature
beyond such practice.

             Pondering that, I see stars
between clouds in a night sky. I smell night-blooming
flowers and the garbage pit on a cool breeze.

               I listen, but
nobody who knows speaks of that.

●

●

Will good and evil deeds be weighed?
Who ponders such nonsense is lost.

Does a farmer eaten by a tiger
mourn the rice he harvested?

If the ugly, filthy feet of the Buddha
protrude from the pyre,

one may snicker softly
as flames tickle the toes

and black smoke rises
in vain to the sun.

●

●

Cold Peak sees with one eye of sun and one eye of moon.

The eye of moon is always full
and rolls through blue in the midst of day.

The eye of sun sparks in darkness
and spins through the night.

He says he sees
the world and the void
at one
and the same time.

And that's exactly the way it appears.

●

●

These poor bald boys are confused about study.
　　　They sit mocking rocks
　　　　　in the stone garden.

　　　Anyone looking sees
　　　　　　who understands
　　as monks rise after meditation.

Most scurry off staring at naked feet. Too many
　　　bob and bow as they creep away.
Some drift along, yearning for the calm of clouds.

　　　These are all lost.

　　Leaving the hall,
　　the good student passes the teacher
　　　　　and goes on.

●

●

My path is clear,
lost in rocks, grass, blossoms, and leaves:

a departure
from trails blazed by others

to icy heights,
blue peaks, swift clouds.

Long gone, those climbers left only the way
they left behind.

Mis-steps, sudden tumbles,
wrong turns, dead ends are all mine.

My path is gone, but the way remains clear:
my destination was elsewhere.

●

●

Sweeping the temple was the work
of long mornings,
a daily offering of crumbs on a gold plate for the god,
the work of a moment.

Sparrows ate the god's food
for many days before
I thrashed him soundly with my broom—

"Will you protect the temple and these silly monks
when food is stolen
beneath your golden nose?"

That night, the monks claimed the god whined
to them in a terrible dream—

"The janitor spanked me
with his broom this morning!"

The head monk trembled to write to the capital
of this sacrilege
for good reason.

The response was quick for those days,
cryptic and unsigned—

"Beat the god, behold the man, learn the ways of the custodian."

●

About the Author

Eric Paul Shaffer's *Living at the Monastery, Working in the Kitchen* is his fourth book of poetry and a companion volume to *Portable Planet*, which was published by Leaping Dog Press in November 2000 and contains poems of Okinawa, Japan, Indonesia, and America. The poems in both books were written during his eight years of living on the edge of Asia.

His first book, *kindling: Poems from Two Poets* (1988), co-authored with James Taylor III, includes a short selection of early poems. *RattleSnake Rider* (1990), his first solo volume, contains poems of California and western America, published as he departed for Japan. Published by Longhand Press, both books are out of print but not out of style. *Instant Mythology* (1999), a lean, blue sampler of poems, was published by Backer Editions.

Shaffer's poetry is anthologized in *The Soul Unearthed* (Tarcher/Putnam, 1996), *Witnessing Earth* (Catamount Press, 1994), *Maui Muses* (forthcoming 2001), and *On Fry Bread & Poetry* (Longhand Press, forthcoming 2001). His poems appear in *ACM, Asylum, Bakunin, Chaminade Literary Review, Chicago Review, Chiron Review, Fish Drum, Japanophile, Prose Ax, Solo, Stick, The Texas Observer, Threepenny Review,* and *William & Mary Review,* among others.

He also edited and wrote an introduction for *How I Read Gertrude Stein,* a study of the works of Stein by Lew Welch, which was published by Grey Fox Press in 1996.

Shaffer is now at work on *Sure Fire,* a new manuscript of poetry focused on Haleakala and Maui, and *The Ring of Deepest Blue,* a book of ryuka, a traditional Okinawan poetry form. He has written two unpublished novels, *Burn & Learn* and *American River Blues,* and this year, he will complete *Root of the Sun,* his third novel, and *A White Car Nation,* a book of short stories, both based on experiences in Japan. Other projects include *Exile in Paradise,* essays on life in Japan, and *The Mirror of Matsuyama,* a play based on a well-known Japanese folktale.

Shaffer lives with his wife Veronica Winegarner at 2,000 feet on the sunset slope of Haleakala, "The House of the Sun," in a place where land rises burning from the sea and all life arrives by wind and wave. A charter member of the Ancient Order of the Fire Gigglers and the "Clear Pool School" of poetry, he rejoices in his good fortune to live within earshot of pheasants, francolins, cardinals, mynas, and mockingbirds, in an age with so much of "the real work" still to be done.

"*Portable Planet* is a marvelous book. I've been following Shaffer's work for years and he is on a definitive upward spiral."   — Jim Harrison, author of *Legends of the Fall, Dalva, The Road Home* and *The Shape of the Journey*

"Eric Paul Shaffer is my favorite poet — more alive than any other so-called living poet. *Portable Planet* is a masterpiece."   — Sara Backer, author of *American Fuji*

"Eric Paul Shaffer is the best poet writing today. *Portable Planet* liberates American poetry from the stuffiness of the Academy and the silliness of the Slam. Here is a book whistling with fresh air, open vistas, and good humor. *Portable Planet* should be made into our next National Park, but hurry and get your copy, before the next administration sells it off! If Walt Whitman had looked under his own boot soles, he would have found Eric Paul Shaffer — and Shaffer would have been giving old Walt a hot foot. This book burns!"
      — John P. O'Grady, author of *Grave Goods: Essays of a Peculiar Nature*

"*Portable Planet* — reminds me of what poetry is about — clear melody with an easy pleasing pace — plain speech — elegant diction — pictorial — makes each place . . . come alive — Okinawa, Japan, Bali, delta country of California — full of the largely arcane detail that makes up most of Earth life — what do we write for but to say I was here at this time at this place & this is how it struck me — a beautiful book —"
      — Albert Saijo, co-author of *Trip Trap: Haiku on the Road* (with Jack Kerouac & Lew Welch)

"Eric Paul Shaffer's poems carry us ever inward and out, where particular stones sprout wings, where solid ground is shaken by the nimble fingers of small gods, and the normal everyday ways of life stay blessedly themselves. These poems are portable, they're the exact same size as the hip pocket of your mind."   — John Kain, author of *Cheater's Paradise*

"Eric Paul Shaffer's *Portable Planet* demonstrates a nomad's sense of place around the Pacific Rim."   — Magda Cregg, editor of *Hey Lew*

"Complex, paradoxical, and intriguing, this is poetry that makes one quite happy that some writers can't keep their mouths shut."
      — Cheri Crenshaw, *Fearless Reviews*

Leaping Dog Press Books

Portable Planet: Poems / Eric Paul Shaffer / LDP Book #1

    Paper: ISBN 1-58775-000-7, $14.95   **PDF:** ISBN 1-58775-001-5, $7.95

All Weekend with the Lights On: Stories / Mark Wisniewski / LDP Book #2

    Paper: ISBN 1-58775-002-3, $14.95   **PDF:** ISBN 1-58775-003-1, $7.95

Living at the Monastery, Working in the Kitchen: Poems / Eric Paul Shaffer / LDP Book #3

    Paper: ISBN 1-58775-004-X, $12.95   **PDF:** ISBN 1-58775-005-8, $6.95

The Double (Doppelangelgänger): An Annotated Novel / Greg Boyd / LDP Book #4

    Cloth, Signed, Limited: ISBN 1-58775-006-6, $29.95

    Paper: ISBN 1-58775-007-4, $14.95   **PDF:** ISBN 1-58775-008-2, $7.95

Ordering Information

Leaping Dog Press books are available in fine bookstores everywhere,
on the Internet at leapingdogpress.com, Amazon.com, BN.com, and Borders.com,
or by writing to Leaping Dog Press, PO Box 222605, Chantilly, VA 20153-2605.

Enclose $3 for postage and handling for the first paperback book,
$1.50 for each additional paperback book.
For PDF orders, include a valid e-mail address.

Virginia residents must also include 4.5% sales tax.

LEAPING DOG
P·R·E·S·S